The Wild World of Animals

Snakes

Cold-Blooded Crawlers

by Becky Olien

Consultant:
Robert T. Mason, Ph.D.
Associate Professor of Zoology
and J.C. Braly Curator of Vertebrates
Oregon State University

Bridgestone Books
an imprint of Capstone Press
Mankato, Minnesota

Bridgestone Books are published by Capstone Press
151 Good Counsel Drive, P.O. Box 669, Mankato, Minnesota 56002
http://www.capstone-press.com

Library of Congress Cataloging-in-Publication Data
Olien, Rebecca.
    Snakes: cold-blooded crawlers/by Becky Olien.
    p. cm.—(The wild world of animals)
    Includes bibliographical references (p. 24) and index.
    Summary: A brief introduction to snakes, describing their physical characteristics,
habitat, young, food, predators, and relationship to people.
    ISBN 0-7368-1138-9
    1. Snakes—Juvenile literature. [1. Snakes.] I. Title. II. Series.
QL666.O6 O38 2002
597.96—dc21   2001003945

Editorial Credits
Megan Schoeneberger, editor; Karen Risch, product planning editor; Linda Clavel,
    cover and interior designer and illustrator; Heidi Schoof, photo researcher

Photo Credits
Gary W. Sargent, 4
Jan W. Jarolan/GeoIMAGERY, 16
Joe McDonald, cover, 12
Joe McDonald/Pictor, 10
Joe McDonald/TOM STACK & ASSOCIATES, 18
Joe McDonald/Visuals Unlimited, 20
Michael Turco, 8
PhotoDisc, Inc., 1, 6, (texture) cover, 2, 3, 8, 10, 12, 14, 20, 22, 23, 24
Rob and Ann Simpson, 14

1 2 3 4 5 6 07 06 05 04 03 02

Table of Contents

scales

forked tongue

eye

young black rat snake

Snakes

Snakes are long, thin animals without legs. All snakes have forked tongues. They use their tongues to smell. Snakes have jaws that can open wide. Scales cover snakes' bodies. Clear scales cover their eyes.

forked tongue
a tongue that is split in two at the end

mangrove snake

scutes

Snakes Are Reptiles

Reptiles have backbones and use lungs to breathe. All reptiles are cold-blooded. They move in and out of the sun to change their body temperature. Reptiles have thin, leathery scales. Snakes use wide scales called scutes to grip the ground as they move.

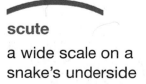

scute

a wide scale on a snake's underside

eyelash viper

A Snake's Habitat

Snakes have habitats all around the world. Many snakes live in grasslands and prairies. Some snakes make their home on the branches of trees in rain forests. Other snakes spend their lives swimming in oceans. Some snakes live underground.

habitat
the place where
an animal lives

gaboon viper

Hunting for Food

Snakes are predators. They hunt other animals for food. Most snakes eat mice, frogs, and lizards. Large snakes sometimes hunt large animals such as crocodiles and antelope. Snakes open their jaws wide around prey. They then swallow the prey without chewing.

antelope

an animal that looks like a large deer and runs very fast

timber rattlesnake

FUN FACTS

Snake venom is used to make medicine called antivenin. It saves people who are bitten by a venomous snake.

Venomous Snakes

Some snakes use venom to kill their prey. Glands in the back of a snake's head hold venom. Venomous snakes have two long, hollow teeth called fangs. Venom flows through the fangs when the snake bites. Rattlesnakes use venom to kill their prey.

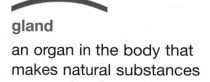

gland

an organic in the body that makes natural substances

southern copperhead

Snakes in Danger

Snakes have many predators. Foxes, raccoons, and birds eat snakes. Some snakes eat other snakes. Many snakes have camouflage to help them hide from predators. Other snakes are brightly colored. The bright colors tell predators to stay away.

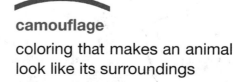

camouflage
coloring that makes an animal look like its surroundings

burmese pythons

Mating and Birth

Most snakes mate in the spring. Other snakes mate in the fall. Female snakes attract male snakes with smells called pheromones. Some female snakes give birth to live young. Other female snakes lay eggs. Snake eggs are soft and stretchy.

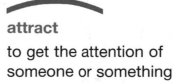

attract
to get the attention of
someone or something

Florida water snake

Shedding *Skin*

A snake molts when it outgrows its skin. A new skin grows under the old one. The color of the snake's skin turns dull. Its eyes become cloudy. The snake crawls headfirst out of its old skin. Young snakes molt every few months. Older snakes molt at least twice a year.

molt
to shed an outer layer of skin

ball python

FUN FACTS

Many people
keep snakes
as pets.

Snakes and People

People often kill snakes for no reason. Many people are afraid of snakes. But snakes aid farmers. They eat small animals that feed on crops. Snake venom can help people. It is used in some medicines.

Hands On: Rattlesnake Rattle

A rattlesnake shakes its rattle as a warning before it bites. A snake's rattle is made of pieces of dried skin. The pieces beat together when shaken to make a buzzing sound. The rattle becomes louder the faster the snake shakes its tail.

What You Need

Pencil
3 small paper cups
Masking tape

What You Do

1. Poke the pencil through the bottom of a paper cup.
2. Push the cup to the eraser end of the pencil.
3. Poke the pencil through the bottom of a second cup.
4. Push this cup up so it is part way under the first cup.
5. Add the last cup in the same way so that it is partly under the middle cup.
6. Wrap masking tape around the pencil point so it will not poke you.
7. Hold the pencil by the taped end and shake it.

The cups work like the sections of a rattlesnake's tail. Shaking the rattle faster and slower makes the sound change.

Words to Know

camouflage (KAM-uh-flahzh)—coloring that makes an animal look like its surroundings

fang (FANG)—a long, sharp tooth; venom flows through fangs.

molt (MOHLT)—to shed an outer layer of skin; snakes molt so they can grow.

pheromone (FER-uh-mohn)—smell produced by an animal; pheromones get stronger when snakes are ready to mate.

predator (PRED-uh-tur)—an animal that hunts and eats other animals

scale (SKALE)—a small, hard plate that covers the body of a snake

venom (VEN-uhm)—dangerous liquid made by some animals

Read More

Behler, Deborah A., and John Behler. *Snakes.*
Animalways. New York: Benchmark Books, 2001.
Montgomery, Sy. *The Snake Scientist.* Boston: Houghton
Mifflin, 1999.
Stille, Darlene R. *Snakes.* First Reports. Minneapolis:
Compass Point Books, 2001.

Internet Sites

All about Nature—Snake Printouts
http://www.enchantedlearning.com/subjects/
reptiles/snakes/printouts.shtml
The Virtual Zoo—Snake
http://library.thinkquest.org/11922/reptiles/
snakes.htm?tqskip=1

Index